Bitcoins and Blockchain: Can Cryptocurrencies perform like Traditional Money?

Julian Dressler

Bibliographic information published by the German National Library:

The German National Library lists this publication in the National Bibliography; detailed bibliographic data are available on the Internet at http://dnb.dnb.de.

ISBN: 9783346478542
This book is also available as an ebook.

© GRIN Publishing GmbH
Nymphenburger Straße 86
80636 München

Print and binding: Books on Demand GmbH, Norderstedt, Germany
Printed on acid-free paper from responsible sources.

GRIN web shop: https://www.grin.com/document/1075960

„Bitcoins and Blockchain": Can Cryptocurrencies perform like
Traditional Money?

Name: Julian Dressler

Words: 2157

Table of Contents

1. List of Figures

2. Abbreviations

CBDC	Central Bank Digital Coin
DLT	Distributed Ledger Technology
ECB	European Central Bank
P2P	Peer to Peer

3. Introduction

Very recently China announced restrictions for its financial institutions to establish a market for cryptocurrencies like bitcoin. As a result, global trading prices for Bitcoin sharply declined about 23% in one week. Figure 1 shows the decline from around 56.000$ at 13th may to around 43.000$ one-week later[21].

Figure 1: "Bitcoin tumbles after China warns on cryptocurrencies"

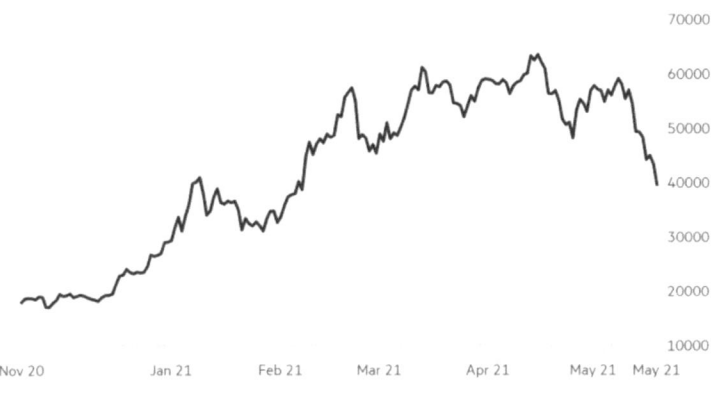

$ per coin

Source: Bloomberg

Source: Hale and Kinder, 19.5.21, last accessed 19.5.21; Bloomberg in Financial Times[21]

In addition, Tesla's announcement to stop accepting Bitcoin for payments, due to its huge negative environmental impact, influenced Bitcoin's decrease in price as well[37,39]. Both events show Bitcoins strong volatility as well as the current hurdles, the cryptocurrency faces to be globally accepted as a method for payment.

At the same time there is an increasing trend in the use of Bitcoin and other cryptocurrencies for speculation, payments, and an increasing interest in the participation in the decentralized finance (DeFi) market. Large companies like Paypal, Lieferando or A&O Hostels started to accept Bitcoin for payments in the beginning of this year.

4

Thus, it seems as if the borders between cryptocurrencies and fiat money become blurrier. Since the use of cryptocurrencies for payments is increasing while at the same time some countries are trying to restrict its use and develop own digital money, it's unclear if Bitcoin could be considered a new form of money[13, 17]. In this paper, the author will explain the differences between both and try to find an answer to the question if cryptocurrencies can perform like traditional money.

4. What is Money

According to traditional literature as well as modern central banks like the ECB, money need to serve three aspects to be recognized and be widely accepted: means for exchange, store of value and unit of account[22, 27, 29, 36, 44].

Means for exchange implies that today's money is widely accepted to buy and sell goods. The use of the euro for example is regulated by the member states of the euro area[44]. Traditionally, there was not really a "means" for exchange, as people used to barter goods directly in the beginning development of money[22, 27]. Similar ideas exist today, like the app "swap" (formerly "swapper") where users can solely trade goods without a "means for exchange"[47].

One can differentiate three traditional forms of money: commodity money, representative money, and fiat money[27, 44]. Commodity money is usually an object with an intrinsic value, which can therefore be exchanged with other products. Traditional examples are gold coins or shells in some societies[7]. According to the commodity theory, the purchasing power is determined by the exchange value of the commodity[22].

In contrast, representative money is only representative for an underlying commodity, such as gold as it was common in the Goldstandard in the 19th century. While this form of money required a 100% coverage of the underlying commodity, modern fiat money requires no coverage. Modern fiat money has no intrinsic value and is regulated by central financial institutions like the ECB who agree about the use of the currency[27, 20].

Two new forms of money are e-money, where the monetary value is stored in a prepaid card and central bank digital currency (CBDC), which represents some form of digital money[23, 43, 44]. The most current example is the Chinese digital remnibi[21].

The impact of central banks becomes clearer with the second characteristic of money: the store of value. The store of value is characterized by its physical durability and by its purchasing power. The latter can be subject of change in terms of inflation or deflation. Central banks are the only authority to issue money[16, 44]. According to fishers' quantity theory of money, the change in the money supply effects inflation or deflation, which underlines the impact of central banks[19, 27.] Central bank policies aim to secure price stability and thereby securing store of value.

The third characteristic of money is the unit of account which means money is used to value goods and services. Therefore, all units need to be fungible, countable, and divisible. In international monetary policy, fungibility with other currencies is reached by fixed or floating currencies [32].

Last, trust in money and banks is vital for it to fulfill all three aspects[3, 22, 44]. "If central banks were to fail in this endeavor, fiat money would lose its general acceptability as a medium of exchange and its attractiveness as a store of value" (ECB, 2015)[44]. Especially for the e-commerce financial institutions serve as a trusted third party. Apart from trust one also needs to consider the cost for transactions and cost for the establishment of these financial institutions[25].

5. What is Bitcoin

Bitcoin is an open source "digital token" according to ECB[43], that was published during the financial crisis in 2009 by the anonymity Satoshi Nakomoto[25], who also owns most Bitcoins - currently 1.1 million according to blockchainweek.com[45].

To obtain Bitcoin there is the derivative and the original form[25]. The original form is through mining. The person mining the bitcoin can be either a company or an individual but is under no supervision of a governmental institutions like banks are[35]. Bitcoins basic technology is the Blockchain, which is a communication protocol introduced in the 1960s and late 1970s. This protocol allows or restricts certain actions and functions as a public ledger to record transfers of Bitcoins[38]. As the name is suggesting, it consists out of a chain of digital blocks. Each of those blocks contains a certain hash of the previous block, a hash being a code converted by a hashing-algorithm – like the SHA-256 hashing-algorithm for bitcoin. To create new Bitcoins, miners need to solve computations. The new Bitcoin is then added as a new block on the blockchain. Because the calculations become more complex with the existence of more Bitcoin, a larger computational power is needed for the calculation[6]. Today, mining is often combined in cloud mining[5]. In addition, the reward for miners for adding a new block is decreasing every four years - currently it is at 6,25 Bitcoins for every newly created block on the blockchain. This halving causes a fixed supply of 21 million bitcoins which will be reached in 2140. In addition, miners also receive a reward for confirming transactions. Every miner has a copy of the blockchain, which is why the blockchain represents a peer-to-peer network (P2P)[2, 24]. Transactions rely on this distributed ledger technology (DLT), which is often referred to as the "trust engine" (Mersch, 2019)[30] of bitcoin. Each user has also personal Wallet-Addresses, that are embedded on the blockchain if a transaction is being processed. To receive Bitcoin the owner of the wallet retrieves a public-key and to send Bitcoin the user needs the private-key of the wallet[7, 30].

As a difference to stable coins Bitcoins' price is solely regulated by supply and demand and Bitcoin has no intrinsic value[8, 30]. Bitcoin is further exposed to the potential of hacking[43]. Multiple articles also underline the energy consumption of bitcoin caused by the mining process[9, 10, 34, 37, 39]. Figure 2 shows the energy consumption of Bitcoin per Dollars spent in Bitcoin.

Figure 2: Bitcoin's Energy Consumption

Source: Financial Times, 2021, last accessed 30.5.2021[9]

Editor's note: The figure has been removed for copyright reasons.

6. Can Bitcoin perform like Money?

To better compare Money with Bitcoin the author will compare the three characteristics of money with the characteristics of Bitcoin.

To serve as a "medium of exchange" Bitcoin needs to be accepted and used sufficiently. A lot of companies make use of Bitcoin as a medium of exchange, and further even governments are considering using cryptocurrency as an accepted medium of exchange. A recent example is El Salvador, whose president announced that the country will accept Bitcoin as a legal tender, arguing that this would allow most of the population access to the financial infrastructure[18]. Furthermore, Chambers[11] argues, that simply the fact that people make use of Bitcoin for payments underlines its role as a medium of exchange. Bitcoin also comes at much lower transaction cost than money and is much faster, especially for international transactions[11, 26]. Bitcoin is not bound to banks or other financial institutions which makes it possible to transfer Bitcoin at any time[11]. This also includes transactions where the anonymity is very important. Before it got shut down in 2013, the so called "Silk-road" was an online marketplace for illegal goods like weapons or drugs, where Bitcoin was used as the sole medium of exchange [31].

Last, Chambers states that Bitcoin transactions are also more protected against fraud than other transactions, because only the owner of the private key has access to the wallet which makes theft or fraud more difficult. Bitcoin transaction can't be reversed which increases its importance as a medium of exchange. Chambers argues that especially in the e-commerce, sales paid with credit cards are often claimed to be paid by someone else, and thereby forcing the credit-card company to charge back the money of the company. This wouldn't be possible with Bitcoin, since only the owner of each wallet has access to the private key needed for the transfer[11].

However, one can also argue, that the possibility of reversing transaction is necessary to use Bitcoin as a means of exchange[11,26, 46]. Most of the transactions are solely done in the ecommerce and occur often in relation to illegal activities.

While Chambers[11] underlines that the use of Bitcoin for illegal activites is underlining its meaning as a medium of exchange, Lo and Wang[26] are stressing that this means Bitcoin is only accepted in small areas of the economy but never for the major part of the economy.

Miller adds that other offerings to pay in Bitcoin are often "gimmicky" (Miller, 2021)[31]. In comparison to fiat money, there is also no trusted third party for Bitcoin transactions. Bitcoin relies on a peer-to-peer network which contains the possibility that one miner gains more than 50% of the mining power and therefore having a huge influence about Bitcoin transactions[26].

Furthermore, it is important to mention that the supply of Bitcoin is limited which would result in deflation for economies that grow faster than the Bitcoin supply. Bitcoin and especially wallets can also be hacked[1].

Last, Miller argues that the acceptance is not very common in the business world and further prices tend to be set in dollars, and not in Bitcoin[31]. This would be difficult anyway to implement, regarding Bitcoins volatility[26, 39].

Regarding the unit of account, Chambers argues that especially crypto exchanges make use of crypto as a unit of account[11]. Further, the blockchain as its underlying technology functions as a ledger, which stresses even more Bitcoin's function as unit of account. Regarding other cryptos, Bullmann[8] argues, that especially stable coins fulfil the characteristic of unit of account even more, with a much lower volatility.

In contrast, Lo and Wang argue, that even vendors who accept bitcoin often present their prices in dollar instead of Bitcoin, due to its volatility[26]. As recent events had shown, news regarding Bitcoin or even Tweets of Elon Musk can largely influence the price[21, 33, 39]. Further, there is a huge dependency to electricity. According to Marques[28] the hash rate of Bitcoin dropped around 40% following a power outage in Xinjang after a flash flood. This underlines Bitcoin's volatility as well as its limited supply.

The volatility of Bitcoin is also an important factor considering its possible characteristic as a store of value. Yermack[46] states that "most widely traded stocks have volatilities in the range of 20% to 30%, and even very risky stocks rarely

9

exhibit volatility as high as 100%". This makes it quite difficult to treat Bitcoin as a store of value[26, 31, 43]. Further it is not backed by a commodity[26, 43].

On the other side, Baur, Hong and Lee[4] argue that Bitcoin shares some characteristics of gold, like the limited supply and supply of growth through mining. Some Authors even refer to Bitcoin as "digital gold" (Weisenthal and Alloway, 2021)[42]. Further, it can't be supplied endlessly like traditionally money can by central banks or government authorities. Chambers[11] argues that the fact that people are investing into the cryptocurrency makes it likely for Bitcoin to serve as a store of value.

7. Conclusion

To sum up, Bitcoin doesn't fulfill most of the characteristics that money has. It is a very volatile "speculative asset" (ECB, 2020)[42, 43], as the ECB describes it. Weisenthal[41] even states that it's no longer arguable, that Bitcoin is a currency. As he describes it, "the HODLer narrative has won" (Weisenthal, 2021)[41]. It is unclear what Bitcoin's future will look like. An article of the Financial Times states, that the current negative environmental impact[21] will lead to a sustainable change for energy providers[9]. An example for this would be the Bitcoin Mining Council[33]. In addition to the environmental issues there is also the trend of countries developing own digital currencies and restricting the use of Bitcoin[21]. Bitcoin has a huge market capitalisation, which makes it likely for Bitcoin to serve further as a speculative asset[41].

8. References

1. Adriano, A. (2018, June). *Crypto Bubble? An Historical Analysis of Financial Crises—IMF F&D Magazine—June 2018 | Volume 55 | Number 2*. International Monetary Fund. https://www.imf.org/external/pubs/ft/fandd/2018/06/crypto-bubble-historical-analysis-of-financial-crises/adriano.htm

2. Antonopoulos, A. (2017). *Mastering Bitcoin: Unlocking Digital Cryptocurrencies* (2nd edition). O'Reilly UK Ltd.

3. Asmundson, I., & Oner, C. (2012). *What is Money*. 2.

4. Baur, D. G., Hong, K., & Lee, A. D. (2018). Bitcoin: Medium of exchange or speculative assets? *Journal of International Financial Markets, Institutions and Money*, *54*, 177–189. https://doi.org/10.1016/j.intfin.2017.12.004

5. Bhaskar, N. D., & Chuen, D. L. K. (2015). Chapter 3—Bitcoin Mining Technology. In D. Lee Kuo Chuen (Ed.), *Handbook of Digital Currency* (pp. 45–65). Academic Press. https://doi.org/10.1016/B978-0-12-802117-0.00003-5

6. Böhme, R., Christin, N., Edelman, B., & Moore, T. (2015). Bitcoin: Economics, Technology, and Governance. *Journal of Economic Perspectives*, *29*(2), 213–238. https://doi.org/10.1257/jep.29.2.213

7. Bouveret, A., & Haksar, V. (n.d.). *What Are Cryptocurrencies like Bitcoin, Ethereum and Ripple? - Back to Basics—IMF F&D Magazine*. International Monetary Fund. Retrieved May 6, 2021, from

https://www.imf.org/external/pubs/ft/fandd/2018/06/what-are-cryptocurrencies-like-bitcoin/basics.htm

8. Bullmann, D., Klemm, J., & Pinna, A. (2019). *In Search for Stability in Crypto-Assets: Are Stablecoins the Solution?* (SSRN Scholarly Paper ID 3444847). Social Science Research Network.
https://papers.ssrn.com/abstract=3444847

9. Carbon counter: Bitcoin is the ultimate hot investment. (2021, May 8). *Financial Times*. Retrieved May 31, 2021, from
https://www.ft.com/content/f723b7cf-ecbf-438b-83f8-3d315ce6293d

10. Carter, N. (2021, May 5). How Much Energy Does Bitcoin Actually Consume? *Harvard Business Review*. Retrieved May 20, 2021, from
https://hbr.org/2021/05/how-much-energy-does-bitcoin-actually-consume

11. Chambers, C. (n.d.). *Bitcoin Really Is Money, Here's Why*. Forbes. Retrieved May 31, 2021, from
https://www.forbes.com/sites/investor/2019/02/15/bitcoin-really-is-money-heres-why/

12. Davis, J. (n.d.). *The Crypto-Currency*. The New Yorker. Retrieved May 30, 2021, from
https://www.newyorker.com/magazine/2011/10/10/the-crypto-currency

13. Davison, L., & Condon, C. (2021). *Crypto Transfers Over $10,000 Should Be Reported to IRS, Treasury Says—Bloomberg*. Retrieved May

21, 2021, from https://www.bloomberg.com/news/articles/2021-05-20/treasury-calls-for-crypto-transfers-over-10-000-reported-to-irs

14. di Mauro, F., Rüffer, R., & Bunda, I. (2008). *The changing role of the exchange rate in a globalised economy.*

15. Doepke, M., & Schneider, M. (2017). Money as a Unit of Account. *Econometrica, 85*(5), 1537–1574. https://doi.org/10.3982/ECTA11963

16. Durlauf, S., & Blume, L. (Eds.). (2010). *Monetary Economics.* Palgrave Macmillan UK. https://doi.org/10.1057/9780230280854

17. Enright, T. (2021). Bank of England is looking into launching "Britcoin". But what is it? *Euronews.* Retrieved May 22, 2021, from https://www.euronews.com/2021/04/29/bank-of-england-looks-into-launching-its-own-britcoin

18. Feuer, W. (2021, June 7). El Salvador will be first country to adopt bitcoin as legal tender. *New York Post.* Retrieved June 7, 2021, from https://nypost.com/2021/06/07/el-salvador-will-be-first-country-to-adopt-bitcoin-as-legal-tender/

19. Fisher, I. (1911). *The purchasing power of money.* Macmillan.

20. Gobry, P.-E. (2013). All Money Is Fiat Money. *Forbes.* Retrieved June 7, 2021, from https://www.forbes.com/sites/pascalemmanuelgobry/2013/01/08/all-money-is-fiat-money/

21. Hale, T., & Kinder, T. (2021). *Bitcoin falls sharply after China signals crypto crackdown.* Retrieved May 22, 2021, from

https://thefinanceinfo.com/2021/05/19/bitcoin-falls-sharply-after-china-signals-crypto-crackdown/

22. Ingham, G. (2013). *The Nature of Money*. John Wiley & Sons.

23. Kaminska, I. (2021, May 5). *Why CBDCs will likely be ID-based*. Retrieved May 8, 2021, from https://www.ft.com/content/88f47c48-97fe-4df3-854e-0d404a3a5f9a

24. Kroll, J. A., Davey, I. C., & Felten, E. W. (2013). *The Economics of Bitcoin Mining, or Bitcoin in the Presence of Adversaries*. 21.

25. Lerch, M. P. (2015). Bitcoin als Evolution des Geldes: Herausforderungen, Risiken und Regulierungsfragen. *Zeitschrift Für Bankrecht Und Bankwirtschaft*, *27*(3). https://doi.org/10.15375/zbb-2015-0304

26. Lo, S., & Wang, C. (2014). *Bitcoin as Money?* https://www.bostonfed.org/publications/current-policy-perspectives/2014/bitcoin-as-money.aspx

27. Mankiw, N. G. (2013). *Principles of Macroeconomics* (7. Edition). Cengage Learning, Inc.

28. Marques, B. (n.d.). *Bitcoin hashrate drops after coal mine accident in China—Crypto DeFinance*. Retrieved June 7, 2021, from https://www.cryptodefinance.com/bitcoin-hashrate-drops-accident-china/

29. Meikle, S. (1994). *Aristotle on Money*. https://brill.com/view/journals/phro/39/1/article-p26_2.xml

30. Mersch, Y. (2019). *Back to stable*. European Central Bank.

https://www.ecb.europa.eu/press/key/date/2019/html/ecb.sp19052
9~7e037a684b.en.html

31. Miller, R. (n.d.). *Bitcoin Is A Cryptocurrency, But Is It Money?* Forbes.

Retrieved May 31, 2021, from

https://www.forbes.com/sites/rmiller/2021/03/23/bitcoin-is-a-
cryptocurrency-but-is-it-money/

32. Oatley, T. (2009). *International Political Economy: Interests and
Institutions in the Global Economy: United States Edition* (4. Edition).

Routledge Member of the Taylor and Francis Group.

33. Ou, E. (2021, June 5). Elon Musk Is Pulling Bitcoin Where It Loathed to

Go. *Bloomberg.Com*. Retrieved June 6, 2021, from

https://www.bloomberg.com/opinion/articles/2021-06-05/elon-
musk-is-pulling-bitcoin-where-it-loathed-to-go

34. Rininsland, Æ., Kao, J. S., Martin, K., & Nauman, B. (2021, May 20).

Bitcoin's growing energy problem: 'It's a dirty currency.' Retrieved

May 20, 2021, from https://www.ft.com/content/1aecb2db-8f61-
427c-a413-3b929291c8ac

35. Segendorf, B. (2014). What is Bitcoin? *Sveriges Riksbank Economic
Review 2014*. http://archive.riksbank.se/en/Web-
archive/Published/Notices/2014/What-is-Bitcoin/

36. Smithin, J. (2002). *What is Money?* Routledge.

37. Tett, G. (2021). *Elon Musk wakes up to bitcoin's fossil fuel issues*.

Retrieved May 22, 2021, from

https://www.ft.com/content/b917ec4f-8b57-45dc-82ba-960d82ad7974

38. Twesige, R. (2015). *Bitcoin A simple explanation of Bitcoin and Block Chain technology JANUARY 2015 RICHARD LEE TWESIGE*.

    https://doi.org/10.13140/2.1.1385.2486

39. Waters, R. (2021, May 14). Musk well-positioned to steer cryptocurrency's future direction of travel. *Financial Times*. Retrieved June 7, 2021, from https://www.ft.com/content/287f5901-d742-4954-94fb-40ab1255262a

40. Weber, B. (2016). Bitcoin and the legitimacy crisis of money. *Cambridge Journal of Economics*, *40*(1), 17–41.

    https://doi.org/10.1093/cje/beu067

41. Weisenthal, J. (2021). There's a New Vision for Crypto, and It's Wildly Different From Bitcoin. *Bloomberg.Com*. Retrieved June 8, 2021, from https://www.bloomberg.com/news/articles/2021-06-07/bitcoin-btc-vs-ethereum-eth-and-defi-there-s-a-big-difference

42. Weisenthal, J., & Alloway, T. (2021). Transcript: Brian Venturo on the Battle for Semiconductors. *Bloomberg.Com*, 23.

43. *What is bitcoin?* (2020, August 29). [European Central Bank]. European Central Bank. https://www.ecb.europa.eu/explainers/tell-me/html/what-is-bitcoin.en.html

44. *What is money?* (2021, May 3). European Central Bank. https://www.ecb.europa.eu/explainers/tell-me-more/html/what_is_money.en.html

45. Who Owns The Most Bitcoin [2021]—Blockchain Week. (n.d.).

Https://Www.Blockchainweek.Com/. Retrieved May 26, 2021, from

https://www.blockchainweek.com/who-owns-the-most-bitcoin/

46. Yermack, D. (2014). *Is Bitcoin a Real Currency? An Economic Appraisal*

(SSRN Scholarly Paper ID 2361599). Social Science Research Network.

https://doi.org/10.2139/ssrn.2361599

47. Zimmermann, M. (2017, April 17). Tinder für überflüssigen Kram: Das

taugt die App Swapper. *DIE WELT*. Retrieved May 30, 2021, from

https://www.welt.de/wirtschaft/webwelt/article163762120/Was-

taugt-das-Tinder-fuer-ueberfluessigen-Kram.html

9. List of Annex

Figure 1: Hale, T., & Kinder, T. (2021). *Bitcoin falls sharply after China signals crypto crackdown*. Retrieved May22, 2021, from

https://thefinanceinfo.com/2021/05/19/bitcoin-falls-sharply-after-china-signals-crypto-crackdown/

Figure 2: Carbon counter: Bitcoin is the ultimate hot investment. (2021, May 8). *Financial Times*. Retrieved May 31, 2021, from

https://www.ft.com/content/f723b7cf-ecbf-438b-83f8-3d315ce6293d